VisuALS: A Startup Strategic Journey

Russell McGuire

Published by SDG Strategy, LLC, 2021.

VISUALS: A STARTUP STRATEGIC JOURNEY

First edition. February 14, 2021.

Copyright © 2021 Russell McGuire.

ISBN: 978-1393811329

Written by Russell McGuire.

Table of Contents

In memory of Carl Phelps. VisuALS' first customer and a man who taught us much about loving others and creating value even through personal trials.

Introduction: The Startup Strategic Journey

Most startups don't have "chief strategy officers." That's not because strategy doesn't matter to startups, but rather because the startup journey is so full of strategic decision making. Entrepreneurs wear many hats — that is one of the great joys and one of the great burdens of the role. "Chief strategy officer" is merely one of those hats.

That being said, most entrepreneurs don't think of their journey that way. They just want to identify a problem they can solve, successfully launch their solution as a business, and position that business for long-term success. The specific strategic decisions along the way may not even be consciously considered. That's a bit scary.

Given my background in both strategy and startups, I'd like to propose a strategic roadmap for entrepreneurs. This Startup Strategic Journey borrows heavily from both startup and strategy camps. It certainly isn't entirely original.

As a Strategic Journey, it's important that we consider what a strategy is. My definition for a strategy is a framework for accomplishing a goal that makes hard decisions easier. Along the journey, entrepreneurs will (formally or not) establish frameworks that make their future decisions easier. Also, although it's generally dangerous to think of a startup as a young/small version of an established company, there are types of strategies and frameworks that can be borrowed from the corporate world to help startups along their journey.

As a Startup Journey, it's important that we remember what a startup is. Steve Blank defines a startup as a "temporary organization in search of a scalable, repeatable, profitable business model." [1]Steve helped launch the Lean Startup movement popularized by Eric Ries and others. In his book *The Lean Startup*[2], Ries does a great job of describing how startups differ from established businesses and how that translates into a completely different approach to management.

There are three major lessons from that book that I believe apply to strategy development for startups:

1. Startups operate in extreme uncertainty, therefore every strategy and every plan must be viewed as a hypothesis to be tested rather than a truth to be implemented.
2. Those hypotheses are tested by running experiments. Startups learn critical lessons from those experiments. Ries describes the Build-Measure-Learn cycle that startups continually iterate through as they refine or reject and replace their hypotheses. You actually implement (build) a version of the hypothesis, see how well it works (measure), and determine how it could be better (learn).
3. During the startup phase, learning is more important than hitting project targets or financial targets. Looking back on the complete life of any successful venture, the goals accomplished and the money made in the earliest days are dwarfed by later achievements, but beginning the venture on the right path is essential to survival and success.

So, as I describe the process of strategy development for a new venture, keep in mind that all parts of that strategy will remain in flux until the startup is well established. Every strategy and every plan will continue to be a hypothesis being tested and iterated through until we learn what we need to know to set the venture on the right path forward.

Below is the general flow that I have found helps a new venture move from a startup concept to a productive operation. As the discussion above implies, just because there are boxes and arrows doesn't mean that any one of these steps is fully complete before moving to the next. Iteration and refinement will continue, and decisions made in a later step very likely will result in re-examining a strategy or plan developed in an earlier step. That being said, this chart represents the general order in which different strategies are developed and decisions are made.

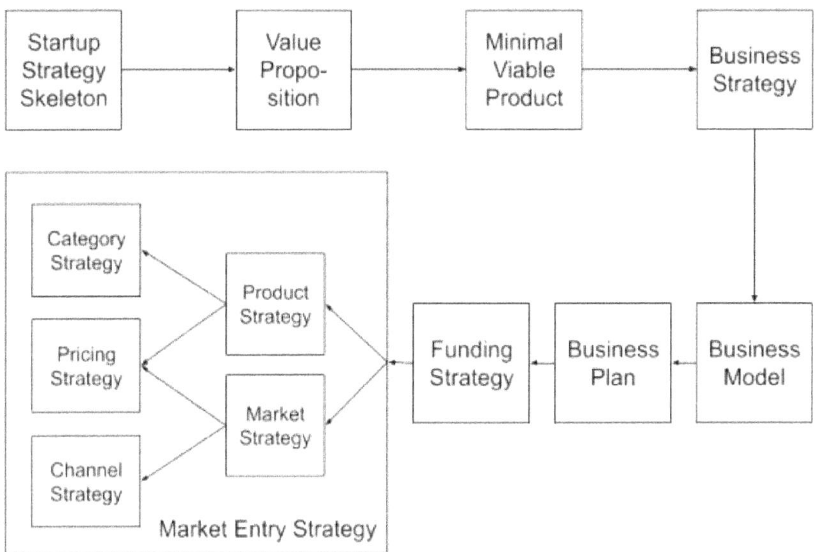

Figure 1: The Startup Strategic Journey

In the following chapters we will discuss each of the steps in the Startup Strategic Journey represented by a box in the above diagram. We will also specifically follow along as one startup, VisuALS Technology Solutions, LLC, takes these steps along their strategic journey.

Enjoy the journey!

The Startup Strategy Skeleton

Ash Srinivas' friend Weyton received the heartbreaking diagnosis. He had Amyotrophic Lateral Sclerosis (ALS) also known as Lou Gehrig's disease. As a doctor, Weyton knew the prognosis. ALS is a fatal disease that slowly takes away your ability to function as the brain loses the ability to communicate with different parts of the body. Early in the disease's progression, Weyton lost lower body strength, then the use of his arms and hands, and finally the ability to speak clearly and audibly. There was no longer a way for him to easily communicate with those he loved.

Thankfully, scientists and engineers have created technology to enable patients like Weyton to communicate by "typing" messages by looking at the letter keys on an on-screen keyboard (eye gaze) and then having the computer speak what has been "typed" (text-to-speech). The device that Weyton received was priced at nearly $20,000 but he had good insurance coverage which would cover most of the cost.

In addition to being Weyton's friend, Ash was also a mobile technology developer. He knew that there was no reason for the device that Weyton used to cost $20,000. His friend could afford it, but Ash knew that many others couldn't and therefore would be "locked in" — cut off from the world around them. Ash was also a student in the Master of Science in Engineering program at Oklahoma Christian University (OC). He approached Steve Maher, chair of the graduate engineering program at OC to see if there might be an opportunity for students to explore creating a lower cost alternative.

Steve also teaches in the undergraduate program at OC and is one of the advisors for electrical and computer engineering student capstone projects — a three-semester systems-level engineering program that each undergraduate engineering student must complete before graduating. Over the years, Steve and his wife have also been involved in helping those with special needs. The problem, or rather opportunity, that Ash presented was one that touched Steve's heart and he knew that it would touch those of some of the students at OC. He was able to quickly get a student team assigned to explore the potential of meeting this need.

Figure 2: Daniel, Allison, and Drew working with Weyton

Students Allison Chilton, Daniel Griffin, and Drew Harris began work on a concept that would lead to a startup called VisuALS Technology Solutions, LLC.

Startup Strategy Skeleton

NEW VENTURES EXIST to apply a new solution to a known problem. Documenting this as the most basic strategy for the startup is the first step in the Startup Strategy Journey.

There are three critical elements that make up the Startup Strategy Skeleton:

- **Problem:** What problem are you trying to solve? Who has this problem?
- **Solution:** What is the new solution that you are bringing to solve the problem?
- **Money:** Where does the money come from? For a business, how will it make money? For a non-profit, what are the sources of funding?

Although it is essential to identify these three elements of the startup strategy, new ventures often change at least one of these elements before successfully launching.

In *Value Proposition Design*[3], Alex Osterwalder and his co-authors suggested using a "mad lib" approach to identifying the problem and solution. They specifically recommended filling in the blanks to complete this sentence:

> *Our [products and services] help(s) [customer segment] who want to [jobs to be done] by [verb] and [verb] (unlike [other existing solution]).*

A simple sentence in this form captures the Problem and Solution elements of the Startup Strategy Skeleton.

The third element is an identification of who will see value in the solution and be willing to pay for it. Sometimes, this is clear. If opening a restaurant, it is reasonable to expect that diners will pay for the food they eat. But for many startups, there may be much learning before the revenue model is finalized.

When thinking about the revenue model, there are three dimensions worth considering:

- What is the nature of the value (product, service, information/

content, financial)?

- How will people pay (one time, flat rate recurring, usage based, value based)?
- Who will pay you (end customers/retail, middle men/ wholesale, third parties/2-sided[4])?

Many businesses may combine multiple revenue models in their business. For example, an auto repair shop will sell parts (products) for a fixed fee, will sell services on a usage based model (per hour), may sell an extended warranty (a form of information), and may even get paid a marketing fee by Quaker State for promoting their brand of oil (third party/2-sided).

Many non-profits also have multiple revenue models, including being paid some directly by those they serve, selling products or services in fundraiser events, and receiving donations from third-parties. However, at this stage in strategy development, it's best to keep your revenue model as simple as possible.

VisuALS' Startup Strategy Skeleton

THE CONCEPT THAT WOULD become VisuALS started with a pretty straightforward idea.

Their Startup Strategy Skeleton can be summarized as:

- **Problem:** Existing eye gaze-based augmentative/alternative communications (AAC) solutions are too expensive.
- **Solution:** Combine available off-the-shelf hardware components with new student-developed proprietary software to design, build, and sell a more affordable solution.
- **Money:** Families of ALS patients will purchase these systems.

In the following chapters we will hear more of the story of how teams, starting with this initial concept, walked through the startup strategy journey to launch a product and a business that is still restoring independence, dignity, and hope for families across America today.

VisuALS' Value Proposition

In the previous chapter I shared how a team of students at Oklahoma Christian University (OC), inspired by ALS-stricken Weyton, took up the challenge of developing a lower-cost solution for ALS patients to be able to communicate with their loved ones.

The team interacted with Weyton, other ALS patients at a monthly ALS Support Group, and with professionals with the ALS Association, the Muscular Dystrophy Association, and the Neuromuscular Disease Clinic at a local hospital. That team developed an initial prototype and received feedback on what changes were required to make it a viable product.

That first team of students had completed their three-semester project and they were graduating. So they handed the concept off to a new team of four seniors to work as their capstone project. The two teams interacted together with those in the ALS community and then the handoff was complete. More than anything, the new group of students listened to what ALS patients really needed.

The Value Proposition

DURING THE ITERATIVE, hypothesis-testing, learning-focused Lean Startup process, new ventures typically move through three phases of validation:

- **Problem-Solution Fit:** You know that potential customers have a specific problem and you have designed a solution that addresses that problem.
- **Product-Market Fit:** The products and services that make up

your solution have demonstrated that they are creating
compelling value, resulting in meaningful traction in the
market.

- **Business Model Fit:** You have successfully created a scalable
and profitable business model around your solution.

Achieving Problem-Solution Fit can be reflected in a well-documented
value proposition.

In *Value Proposition Design*[5], a value proposition is defined as
describing, "the benefits customers can expect from your products and
services." The authors of that book provided a very helpful tool, the Value
Proposition Canvas[6], for developing and capturing a value proposition.

Developing a valid value proposition is not an afternoon brainstorming
exercise on a whiteboard in a conference room. Steve Blank's mantra
of "get out of the building" is critical. You need to spend time deeply
understanding the customer, and you need to test many different
potential value propositions to learn which will actually solve the
problem and create value for the customer.

Understanding the customer typically involves observing them and
talking to them. A good conversation isn't a survey where you ask them
direct and leading questions about what you think their problem is;
instead it may start with asking them what a typical day is like for them.
You want to understand the "jobs" they do throughout the day, and
which ones are really important. You want to understand why they do
what they do — what they hope to get out of the activities they do. You
also want to understand what is hard about what they do — what are the
problems.

Once you uncover an interesting problem, you want to probe to learn
what they've previously done to try to solve the problem. For each

potential solution they've tried (which might be another company's product, or it might be something they've done themselves), you want to understand what was good about that solution and what was disappointing. Assuming they still have the problem (or else it wouldn't have come up), you want to understand why the solution they tried hasn't solved the problem.

This is a conversation you want to have as many times as possible with as many different people as possible. From these discussions, you may find that the problem you thought certain people had isn't really a problem. You might modify your startup strategy to address a different problem (and a different solution). Or you might find that it's a different group of people with the problem. Or, at this point, you might abandon the new venture altogether.

Testing potential solutions/value propositions also involves getting out of the building and interacting with potential customers. It is critical that value proposition testing not be mixed into the customer exploration process. Once you introduce a potential solution, the customer's ability to independently describe their situation will be derailed and they will only focus on your potential solution.

Theoretically, it is possible, at the very end of the same discussion with the customer, once you've fully explored their situation, to introduce your potential solution and get their reaction. However, when that's our plan, our nature is to rush to get to the part of the discussion where we can talk about our concept. To avoid that temptation, it is best to, if appropriate, ask the person at the very end of the conversation if they'd like to schedule a follow-up conversation to hear about your solution.

In *The Startup Mixtape*[7], Elliott Adams advocates using prototypes to learn from customers whether your proposed solution will truly solve their problem and create value. He describes a prototype as "a representation of the final product experience that conveys the value of the solution you plan to offer your customers." Early prototypes probably won't be working models of the solution, but may be more like marketing materials — a web page describing the features and benefits or maybe even an explainer video telling the story and walking through what the product will do. Simple mock-ups of what the product might look like can be helpful. If you're building a physical product, a 3D-printed model may also help the customer envision your solution and be able to react to it.

In the end, you are looking for their honest reaction. Does the solution that you're proposing help them achieve what they want while eliminating the challenges, roadblocks, and pains that are keeping them from achieving that goal?

Once you have deeply understood and documented the customer, and identified a solution (value proposition) that solves the customer's problem and creates value for them, then you have achieved Problem-Solution Fit and can move forward.

VisuALS' Value Proposition

BASED ON THEIR DISCUSSIONS with the ALS community, and the lessons passed on from the first team, the new team developed a solid understanding of the value proposition and target customer as represented in this Value Proposition Canvas.

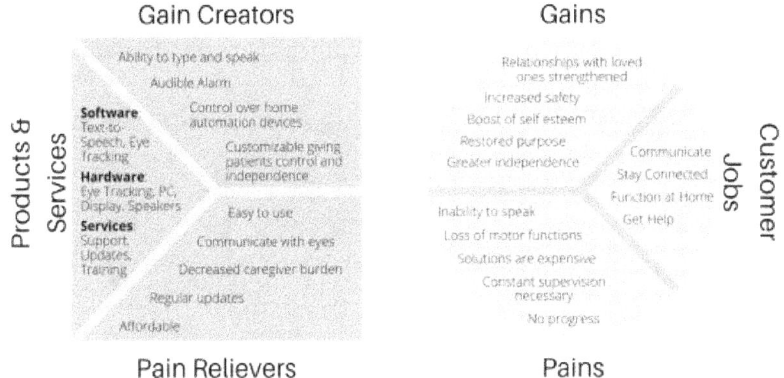

Figure 3: VisuALS Value Proposition Canvas

Over time, many ALS patients will lose the ability to speak and to use their hands. This makes it almost impossible for them to positively engage with the world around them. Most importantly, they want to communicate with those they love. They want to stay connected with their community. They want to be able to have some level of control over their environment (e.g. turning on lights, changing the TV channel). And at times, they need to get the attention of caregivers.

Sadly, ALS is a degenerative disease and there is not yet a cure. As I previously mentioned, there already were solutions on the market, but most of those products seemed priced to maximize payments from insurance companies rather than being affordable for families.

The students knew enough from the work that the first team had done and the additional experimentation that they were doing, to know that they could build a much more affordable solution with off-the-shelf hardware and new software they were developing. Text-to-speech would allow the patient to speak with their loved ones. Simple home automation would further increase independence for the patients.

Controlling a web browser and e-mail client likely could be developed in the future to enable staying connected with distant friends and family.

Based on their discussions, the team felt ready to take it to the next step — the Minimal Viable Product.

VisuALS' Minimal Viable Product

In the previous chapter we saw how the VisuALS student team listened to the ALS community and developed their Value Proposition. They believed they had Problem-Solution fit. But to get to Product-Market fit, they needed to get the product into customers' hands and start truly learning.

Minimal Viable Product

IT'S NATURAL TO WANT to wait until a product has enough features and finish to be something you'd be proud of before giving it to customers, but that is a dangerous temptation. The old saying is, "perfect is the enemy of good," but in the Lean Startup model, "good is the enemy of now." Reid Hoffman, co-founder of LinkedIn famously said, "If you're not embarrassed by the first version of your product, you've launched too late."[8]

The real goal is to spend as little time and as little money as possible to get something into the hands of a few customers that demonstrates the very core of your value proposition. In Lean terms, this is your Minimal Viable Product (or MVP). It typically won't have as many features as the prototypes that you have shown to customers, but it will be a real product and not just a mock up. Elliott Adams says that an MVP should be valuable, usable, and feasible. By valuable and usable, he means that customers can actually start using your MVP in trying to address their issues, and it does enough in helping them that they want to use it. By feasible, he means that it's something that you can quickly get to market in a form that you can continue to improve. That probably means that you have the people and tools to build it within your company and won't have to outsource to an expensive third party.

Given the nature of an MVP, it is critical to choose the right customers to give it to. Blank and Dorf[9] refer to this type of customer as an *Earlyvangelist* — someone who knows they have the problem, have been actively looking for a solution, and have been so desperate to find one that they have tried cobbling together something themselves until they can find a real solution. These types of customers will appreciate your vision, will tolerate the roughness of your early iterations, and will partner with you to improve your product until it truly solves their problem.

To be clear, the goal of an MVP is NOT to convince customers that you have the right final solution for them, but rather to learn from customers how to iterate from what you have to what they really need — or to learn that you need to go back to the drawing board and identify a different solution. As you iterate from your MVP towards a truly market-ready product, you can begin to expand the number and types of customers who are using your product.

Product-Market Fit happens when the market is excited about your solution and an increasing number of customers are willing to pay a fair market price to purchase it. There's no magic metric that defines when you've reached Product-Market Fit, but some describe it in terms of there being more demand than you can keep up with or needing to hire sales and support people as fast as you can.

VisuALS' Minimal Viable Product

AT THIS POINT, THE student team was made up of four Oklahoma Christian University (OC) Electrical or Computer Engineering students, Josh Bilello, Aubrey Gonzalez, Preston Kemp, and Tyler Sriver.

They were good at building stuff. They also were compassionate, caring deeply about the plight of ALS patients and wanting to help. But they lacked business knowledge. At the time I was serving as Entrepreneur in Residence at OC, so I came alongside the team and helped them recruit Jevon Seaman, an accounting student, and Kevin McGuire (my son), a marketing student. With myself and Steve Maher, the extended team was now up to eight.

Figure 4: Kevin, Preston, Aubrey, Tyler, Josh, and Jevon

In December 2016 the team had the basic functionality working. They were scared to let "real" users try it because they knew where all the bugs were and it was missing some pretty important functionality. But Steve convinced them to take it to the monthly ALS Support Group meeting at a local hospital.

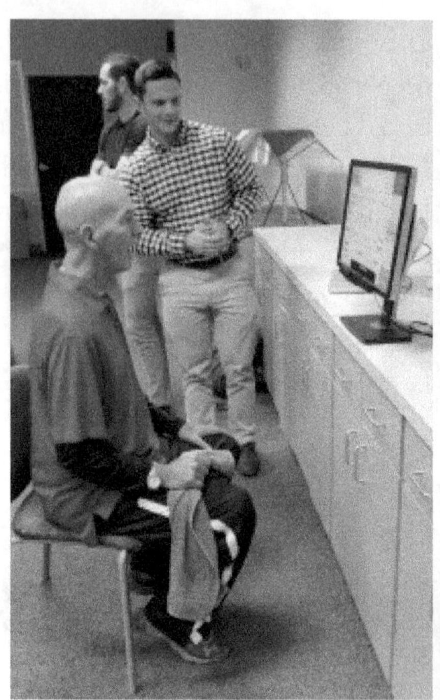

Figure 5: Preston Helps Carl with VisuALS

After the meeting started, the coordinator introduced Steve who quickly handed it over to the team. While Josh explained the goal of their project and what they'd been able to accomplish, one of the patients stood up and made his way over to where the system was set up. Preston stepped aside so the patient could sit down in front of the VisuALS system. As Josh continued to talk, Preston helped Carl get calibrated to the eye gaze hardware.

The first words he typed with his eyes were "I love you Janice." Carl hadn't been able to speak those words to his wife for about a year. He was losing control over his hands, and within just a couple of months we would only see him in a wheelchair. For the next 45 minutes Carl continued to speak through the VisuALS system — asking the students questions and making suggestions. Well after the meeting had officially ended, Carl said "I'm not giving this back until you tell me when I can have my own."

ALS is a fatal disease. As they left the room, Janice said "you may not have long."

The next day the students met to discuss how they could get a system for Carl to use. They used the rest of their project budget to order some needed components and called Janice. Three weeks later they drove for an hour down I-44 to Carl and Janice's home in Chickasha, Oklahoma. They were greeted with love and gratitude. The students' lives were changed forever.

Carl wore the title of "beta tester" with pride. And he earned it! Carl was constantly using the system and providing feedback. Before delivering the system, the team had been able to develop one of Carl's requests from his first session three weeks before. They continued to iterate and refine the MVP. After a few weeks, the university sent a video crew with the team to visit Carl. The video they produced can be viewed at https://youtu.be/CeJtSLkCD58

The team continued to attend ALS Support Group meetings in Oklahoma City and Tulsa and got systems into the hands of more ALS patients who also provided feedback. Not only were they learning what the product needed, but they were beginning to understand what a business would need to provide and support VisuALS systems for those in need.

Next stop — the Business Strategy.

VisuALS' Business Strategy

In the last chapter we heard how VisuALS' Minimal Viable Product (MVP) helped them iterate towards a market-ready product. In this chapter we shift our focus from the product to the business.

By early 2017, the team had decided to enter the Love's Entrepreneur's Cup[1] business plan competition run by i2E[2]. Before they could begin working on their business plan, they needed to understand their business strategy. I facilitated a mini strategy lab to nail down the purpose and pillars of their strategy.

Business Strategy

BUSINESS STRATEGY IS the top-level strategy for a stand-alone business like VisuALS or for a business unit within a corporation. The business strategy will reflect a competitive market and an envisioned future role within that market. Business strategy drives investment decisions in sales/distribution, product development, and operations.

As with other strategies, the Purpose Pyramid can help in developing and communicating a business strategy. The pyramid has four main sections:

- **The Panorama:** The external (opportunities and threats) and internal (strengths and weaknesses) realities within which the strategy is being developed.
- **The Purpose:** A single, brief statement that captures the essence of what your organization is all about — what you aspire to and what you want to be known for.

---

1. https://i2e.org/loves-cup/

2. https://i2e.org/about-i2e/

- **The Pillars:** The three critical realities necessary for your organization's purpose to be achieved.
- **The Plans:** Three very specific tangible actions you are taking to establish and strengthen each pillar (for a total of nine plans).

Getting the Purpose and Pillars right is the hardest and most important aspect of developing a sound strategy. The right Purpose will be uniquely true for your business. It will be memorable and impactful. The right Pillars will focus your efforts on everything required to succeed in achieving your Purpose. If you've identified the right Pillars, then failing to make any one of the Pillars true will very likely lead to failure, while achieving all of the Pillars will very likely lead to success in achieving your Purpose.

VisuALS Business Strategy

GIVEN THEIR PROJECT assignment, the engineering student team had appropriately developed a mission statement that was focused on *product* requirements. The first thing the broadened team needed to do was think *beyond* the initial product. What was true about their passions, their capabilities, the competitive market, and the needs of those they hoped to serve?

The new Purpose they identified was: **Love our neighbors by restoring independence, dignity, and hope through affordable assistive technology solutions.**

Although a little long by my standards, this statement succinctly captures their motivation (Christian love), the impact they wanted to make (restoring independence, dignity, and hope), the market they wanted to serve (those needing assistive technology), their product/service focus (integrated assistive technology solutions), and their competitive positioning (affordability).

Based on their discussions, especially with support organizations, they recognized that there were needs beyond just the ALS community that they could serve (e.g. other degenerative diseases, stroke victims, and those with spinal cord injuries). They also had learned that what their customers needed, more than a communications gadget, was holistic restoration of their participation in life and community.

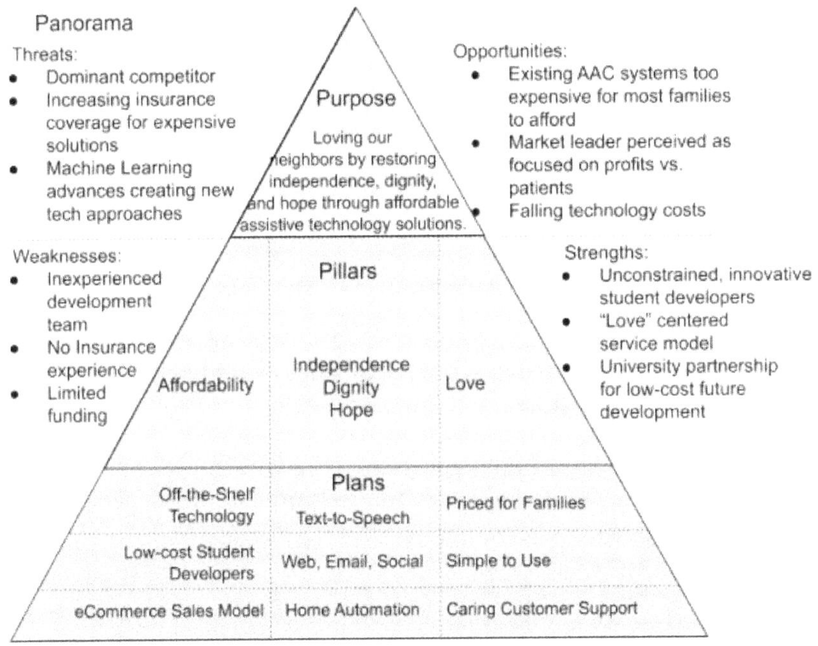

Figure 6: VisuALS' Business Strategy

The team identified three pillars that would guide all future development, whether it would be of their current Augmentative and Alternative Communications (AAC) technology or future developments in mobility, vision, cognition, accessibility, grooming, eating, or any other area of assistive technology. They recognized that future electrical, computer, or mechanical engineering capstone projects at Oklahoma Christian University (OC) could be well suited to adding to the VisuALS product portfolio. The right strategic framework would provide guidance for these future projects that would enable successful integration into a cohesive family of solutions.

At its core, the strategy was focused on restoring independence, dignity, and hope. Feature development investments would be focused on capabilities that enabled wholeness in daily life and loving relationships.

However, the two areas of focus that would set VisuALS apart from competitors were delivering a compellingly affordable solution and operating with love and compassion for their neighbors.

They then identified the three highest priority Plans to establish each Pillar.

The affordability Pillar rested on the successful integration of off-the-shelf technologies so as to avoid the cost of "reinventing the wheel." This Pillar also leveraged the "free" labor of student project teams and the low cost labor of student interns. Finally, compelling affordability required a radically different sales model than competitors used. The business' ability to succeed in its purpose was dependent on successfully establishing e-commerce as a viable channel for assistive technology.

While the long-term strategy envisioned multiple products, the immediate feature Plans focused on core communications and home automation capabilities enabled through the eye gaze interface in the initial product.

Love can be a challenging Pillar to translate into tangible Plans, but the team identified three specific areas of focus to demonstrate unique understanding and compassion. The first was a pricing approach that anticipated the challenges faced by families already stretched by mounting medical bills. Beyond simple affordability, the team developed plans for a crowd-funding component and a compassion donation fund to help the most challenged families. Patients had also commented on the challenges of dealing with products that focused more on feature bragging rights than on simple usability. VisuALS developed plans for radical ease of use. Finally, the team needed to develop plans for customer support that would focus less on operational efficiency and more on compassionate care.

As the team transitioned from Business Strategy into specific plans, the Business Model started to take shape.

VisuALS' Business Model

In the previous two chapters we've seen how the VisuALS team defined their value proposition and their business strategy. In this chapter we will see how they filled out the rest of their business model.

Alexander Osterwalder defines a business model as, "a representation of how an organization makes (or intends to make) money." Making money involves bringing in more money than you're spending, so it's helpful to think of a business model as addressing these two factors:

- What causes money to flow into the business? This is closely tied to the value proposition.
- How do we spend money in delivering the value proposition? Are we spending any money not related to the value proposition?

My favorite tool for representing a business model is Osterwalder's Business Model Canvas, first introduced in his book *Business Model Generation*[10].

The Business Model Canvas

THE BUSINESS MODEL Canvas simplifies everything about a business down to nine components on a single sheet of paper. In typical Lean fashion, the contents of those nine boxes start as hypotheses that you iteratively test and refine.

When you look at the canvas (below), there's an obvious break between the top section (business decisions) and the bottom section (the financial impact). Less obviously, the canvas can be broken in half left and right. At the center is the "Value Proposition" and this truly is the core of the business model. I like to call the right half, the "Front End" of the business model, and it represents the decisions made in order to bring that value proposition to market. The left half, or the "Back End" of the business model, represents all the decisions that enable the business to successfully deliver that value proposition to the target customers. Successful execution of the Front End results in the Revenue Streams. Successful execution of the Back End requires investment represented here by the Cost Structure.

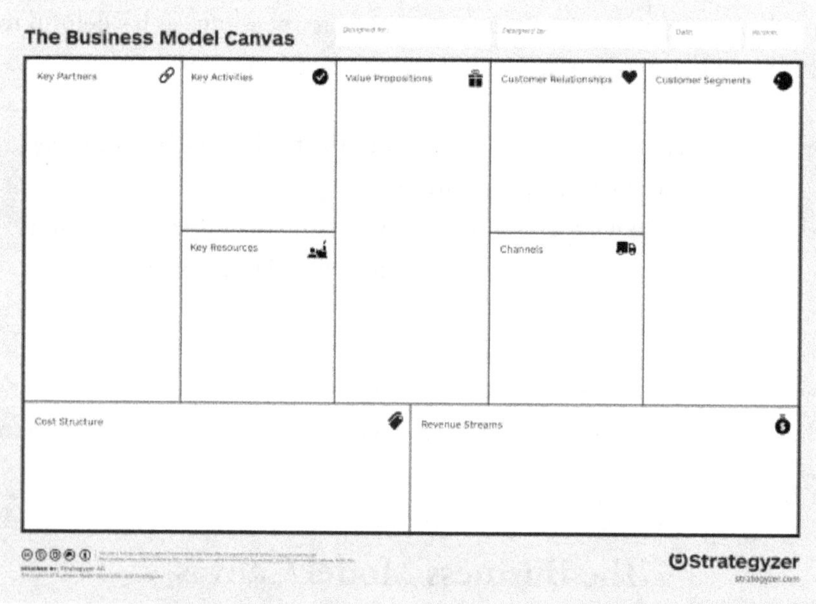

Figure 7: The Business Model Canvas

Looking more closely at the Front End we see two elements that we should already know much about if we've used the value proposition canvas — the Value Proposition and the Customer Segments. The format here is different and so the presentation of the information also needs to adapt. The Value Proposition box should contain a relatively brief summary of how your business creates value for the target customers. If possible, this box can also contain initial hypotheses around different offers and pricing approaches to reflect that value. Similarly, the Customer Segments box contains a relatively brief summary of the target customers and optimally would include market sizing information.

The remaining two boxes in the top portion of the Front End explain the mechanics and relationships involved in growing revenue by delivering the Value Proposition to the Customer Segments. The Channels box represents customer acquisition — what will be your primary marketing and sales channels to bring in new customers? The Customer Relationships box represents customer retention — what will you do to maintain a relationship with the customer to bring in future revenue from each customer?

The Revenue Streams box captures the net result of the four Front End boxes. The success of the Channels will determine how quickly sales grow while successful management of Customer Relationships will result in ongoing recurring revenues and/or follow-on sales.

The heart of the Back End is the column with the Key Activities and Key Resources required to deliver the Value Proposition to the Customer Segments. In other words, what do you need to do (activities) and what do you need to have (resources) in order to operate the business. It's unlikely that a new venture will have all the resources and capabilities required, so the Key Partners box identifies key vendors and alliance partners who will help fill in the gaps. It can be helpful to organize these partners into categories aligned with the Key Activities, perhaps sales, marketing, product development, manufacturing, operations, and distribution.

The Cost Structure box reflects the expenses represented by the Back End boxes. Although typically qualitative and not quantitative, optimally this is reflected in terms that will translate well to a financial model — cost of goods, fixed costs, and variable costs.

VisuALS' Business Model Canvas

IN DEVELOPING THEIR business model, the VisuALS team started from the value proposition they had previously developed, the lessons they'd learned through their MVP, and the broader vision they'd developed as part of their business strategy.

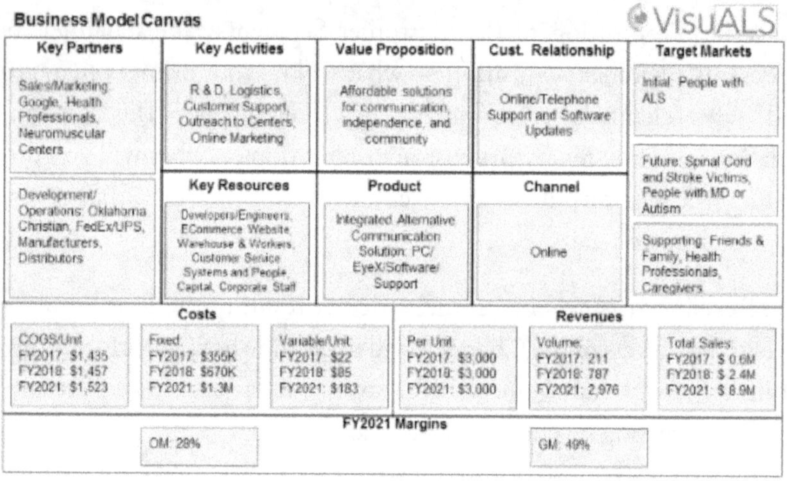

Business Model Canvas — VisuALS

Key Partners	Key Activities	Value Proposition	Cust. Relationship	Target Markets
Sales/Marketing: Google, Health Professionals, Neuromuscular Centers	R & D, Logistics, Customer Support, Outreach to Centers, Online Marketing	Affordable solutions for communication, independence, and community	Online/Telephone Support and Software Updates	Initial: People with ALS
	Key Resources	**Product**	**Channel**	Future: Spinal Cord and Stroke Victims, People with MD or Autism
Development/ Operations: Oklahoma Christian, FedEx/UPS, Manufacturers, Distributors	Developers/Engineers, ECommerce Website, Warehouse & Workers, Customer Service Systems and People, Capital, Corporate Staff	Integrated Alternative Communication Solution: PC/ EyeX/Software/ Support	Online	Supporting: Friends & Family, Health Professionals, Caregivers

Costs			Revenues		
COGS/Unit FY2017: $1,435 FY2018: $1,457 FY2021: $1,523	Fixed FY2017: $355K FY2018: $670K FY2021: $1.3M	Variable/Unit FY2017: $22 FY2018: $85 FY2021: $183	Per Unit FY2017: $3,000 FY2018: $3,000 FY2021: $3,000	Volume FY2017: 211 FY2018: 787 FY2021: 2,976	Total Sales FY2017: $ 0.6M FY2018: $ 2.4M FY2021: $ 8.9M

FY2021 Margins   OM: 28%   GM: 49%

Figure 8: VisuALS' initial business model (numbers are merely illustrative)

Let me point out a few structural notes about how the team adapted the canvas to their needs. Most obviously, there appear to be more than 9 boxes in this canvas. For starters, they decided to include a description of their initial product in the value proposition slot.

They also broke several of the other boxes into multiple components. On the far left, they broke the key partners into those on the "front end" involved in acquiring and maintaining customer relationships, and those on the "back end" involved in developing, building, and delivering the value proposition to customer. On the far right, they wanted to think about target customers in three buckets: the initial target market, future target markets, and those influencing the decision process.

They also handled the financial boxes with more granularity than the standard canvas requires. They looked at three categories of expenses: fixed, cost of goods per unit sold, and other variable costs per unit sold. On the revenue side, they called out the price and volume leading to total revenues. Finally, they added an additional box at the bottom to reflect long-term margins.

Within the remaining boxes we see reflected some of the decisions that went into their business strategy. Because of the focus on affordability, all sales would be online and customer support would be over the phone and online. That meant that, unlike competitors, they wouldn't need a distributed workforce providing in-person sales and support. Given their focus on "loving their neighbors" they would need to make sure that the virtual support personnel were carefully selected and trained. Their partnership with Oklahoma Christian University would also play a key role in maintaining affordability.

The level of detail that went into the business model set the stage for the team to develop their full business plan.

VisuALS' Business Plan

As I mentioned in an earlier chapter, the VisuALS team decided to enter the Love's Entrepreneurs Cup business plan competition. In 2017 the competition had three stages:

- A written business plan, including financial projections, was submitted in early March.
- From the dozens of entries, eight semi-finalist teams were selected. These teams presented to judges in early April.
- Six of the eight semi-finalist teams were selected to advance to the finals and present again the next day to a different set of judges.

The Business Plan

A BUSINESS PLAN DOCUMENT creates a narrative that anyone can pick up and understand. A good business plan should address two critical audiences: potential investors and the venture team themselves.

For investors, the business plan document should address all of the critical factors necessary for the success of the venture. These readers of the plan will read the plan to answer three types of questions about each aspect of the business:

1. Does the management team have a plan?
2. Does the investor believe successful execution of the plan would generate the hoped for results?
3. Does the invsutor believe this management team can successfully execute the plan?

For the management team, the business plan helps keep everyone on the same page. A new venture typically has lots of activity and not enough people. That means that team members are moving at full speed in many directions, often with little time to stop and coordinate. A good business plan clearly communicates what needs to happen for the success of the venture so that everyone can be working in concert.

A business plan typically is developed through two major efforts. The first is the writing of a narrative, addressing important areas of business planning. The second is a financial model projecting future financial performance of the business. The two elements need to be kept closely in sync. If changes are made to the plans described in the narrative, then the financial model needs to reflect those changes.

The narrative largely flows from the Business Model that we discussed in the last chapter. i2E, the organization that runs the Love's Entrepreneurs Cup competition provides a recommended outline that includes the following sections. I think this does a good job covering key areas of the business:

- Executive Summary
- Company Overview and Background
- Products and Technology
- Customer Identification and Validation
- Market Definition
- Competitive Analysis
- Market Positioning
- Marketing Plan
- Distribution Channels/Sales Approach
- Management Team
- Implementation/Operations Plan
- Financials

For the financial model, I strongly recommend building a bottom-up assumptions-driven model for the business. This can be done in Excel or any spreadsheet software. You create a workbook with multiple worksheets (tabs). One (or more) worksheet(s) contain all of the assumptions. Other worksheets calculate revenue and expenses based on these assumptions. Except for the assumptions worksheet(s), no numeric field in any of the other worksheets should contain any numbers, but rather should contain formulas tied to the assumptions. For example, if you expect the cost of an item to increase by 10% each year, then your assumptions page should contain the initial cost of that item and the anticipated rate of cost increases (10%). Those two assumptions would then be referenced on other worksheets to calculate the cost of that item in any given year. I have provided a video tutorial for how to develop a bottom-up assumption-driven financial model at https://medium.com/clearpurpose/
laptop-tutorial-assumption-driven-financial-modeling-816ecd48e3ff

Taking this approach also makes it easy to change your assumptions in one place and have those changes reflected throughout. For example, the number of salespeople will likely be used both in the calculation of expenses and the calculation of revenue. When the assumptions driving the number of salespeople are changed once, the impact on both revenue and expenses would be automatically reflected.

Your assumptions *will* change. Remember, a new venture faces tremendous uncertainty, and as you test and learn, you *will* change your hypotheses. "Hard coding" numbers into the actual financial worksheets almost ensures that you will forget to change one or more cells and the projections you include in your business plan will have mistakes. Using an assumptions worksheet makes it much easier to keep the projections accurate as you make changes. It also makes it easy to run different scenarios, so as you are considering different options, you can quickly see what impact each would have on the funding required and the short-term and long-term financial performance of the venture.

VisuALS' Business Plan

AS THE VISUALS TEAM moved from the business modeling to the business planning stage, the biggest question they had to answer was how they would generate sales.

They were a brand new company. The largest competitor in the eye-tracking-based augmentative and alternative communications (AAC) market controlled 50–75% of the market, had a huge marketing budget, and had sales reps in most major cities across the country. How could VisuALS' message that they had a significantly lower cost solution break through to the audience that needed to hear it?

Based on discussions that the team had with ALS patients and their families and the broader ALS community, they had a sense for how someone deals with the devastating diagnosis of this fatal, degenerative disease.

One of the first things that a patient or family member will do is a simple Google search to learn what the road ahead looks like and what resources might be available to help. The VisuALS team researched the economics around buying Google ads and decided that would be a key element of their marketing strategy.

Doctors who diagnose ALS also do a great job of getting patients and their families plugged into the local support community. The ALS Association (ALSA) and the Muscular Dystrophy Association (MDA) both provide excellent resources in chapters across the country, including regular support group meetings where patients and their families can gather together to share experiences, encourage one another, and love one another.

The VisuALS team decided to take a city-by-city approach to building brand awareness and sales. They would start with one sales rep traveling each month to a different city. The rep would visit with clinics, doctors, and speech language pathologists serving the ALS community in that city and also time their visit to be able to participate in a support group meeting with ALS patients and their families. The VisuALS team and story had already been warmly welcomed by the ALS community in Oklahoma City and Tulsa and they expected to be similarly warmly welcomed across the country.

The team believed that if they could close just one sale in a city, that would establish a visible demonstration and an "earlyvangelist" helping spread the word in that community. The sales rep would continue to communicate with key contacts in each city to ensure that VisuALS would be recommended to patients as their need for an AAC solution grew.

They expected that they would continue to have growing sales in a city for months after they visited, but set an anticipated cap of selling to 10% of the ALS patients in each targeted city. Sadly, new patients are being diagnosed with ALS everyday, so there would be an unending flow of new potential customers. They set a schedule of cities they would target based on the cities with the largest ALS populations and most active communities. They developed a projection for each individual city and developed their overall sales forecast by compiling together those individual city projections.

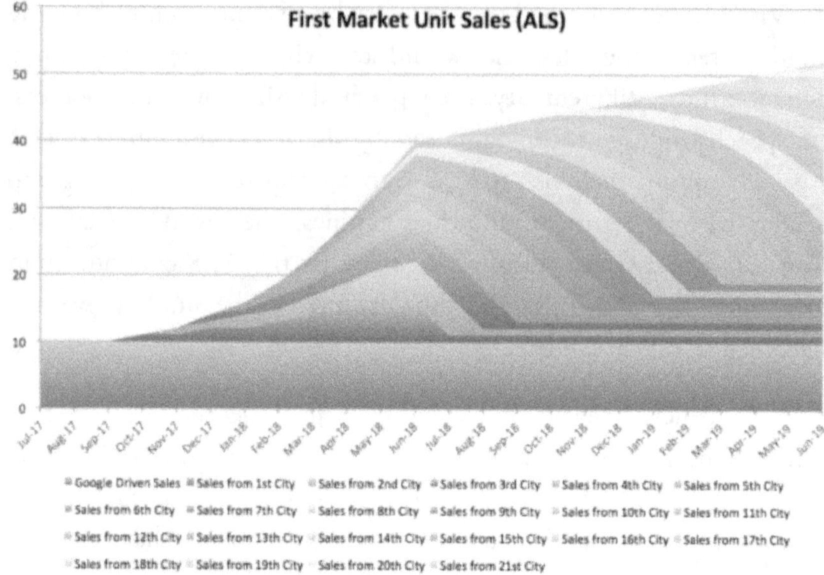

Figure 9: Initial Sales Projections for VisuALS based on city-by-city approach

The team also recognized that their solution would meet the needs of target markets beyond ALS. While their initial focus would be on ALS, they expected to receive orders from non-ALS patients from the beginning. They would develop specific marketing and sales plans for new markets (e.g. stroke victims) and their plan was to pursue an additional market every twelve months.

The team also built a sophisticated bottoms-up financial model. They submitted with their business plan three scenarios run using this model — a baseline plan, an aggressive plan, and a conservative plan.

The judges were apparently impressed with the team's business plan. They advanced to the finals and at the awards ceremony, it was announced that they had won first place (and $11,000) in the small business division.

Figure 10: The VisuALS team receiving their first place award at the Love's Cup awards dinner

The team was excited. But they were also humbled with the responsibility. They had a solution that truly was life-changing. They knew it had to go to market to help many more patients. However, all four of the engineering students were graduating and had committed to employers giving them great jobs to start their engineering careers. It would take time and money to bring the VisuALS product to market.

VisuALS' Funding Strategy

The VisuALS team had won \$11,000 in a business plan competition, but that wasn't going to be enough to launch the business. Perhaps more troubling, most of the team was graduating and had well paying engineering jobs lined up as the first step in their career, what were they going to do?

As you may recall, the VisuALS team had grown from four engineers (Aubrey, Josh, Preston, and Tyler) to include an accounting student (Jevon) and a marketing student (Kevin). The four engineering students were graduating and starting career jobs, with Aubrey and Josh moving out of state. All four wanted to continue as technical advisors. Since Preston and Tyler were staying local, they remained active with the business, working nights and weekends with Tyler becoming chief product officer and Preston becoming chief information officer. Jevon had another year to finish his degree, so he was around campus with more availability. He became chief operating officer along with managing the financials. Professor Steve Maher took on the role of chief technology officer and I took on the role of chief executive officer. We also brought on Austin McRay as chief sales and marketing officer half-time as he continued in a similar role with another Oklahoma Christian University (OC) startup[1].

With summer about to begin, we hired four bright young computer science and engineering students as summer interns to turn the MVP into a market-ready product. We also had to work out all of the operational aspects including becoming an approved reseller of the hardware components, establishing inventory, implementing logistics and customer support processes, and more. Our goal was to officially

---

1. https://medium.com/clearpurpose/my-startup-journey-altimeter-software-78b849baa990

launch the product on September 1, 2017 and we had a lot of work to do. More urgently, we needed money to do much of that work.

Funding Strategy

THERE ARE MANY FORMS of funding and the right funding strategy may change throughout the life of a venture. Entire books are written on funding new ventures, so I won't try to cover all the details here. Two books I would recommend are *Get Backed*[11] by Evan Baehr and Evan Loomis and *Venture Deals*[12] by Brad Feld and Jason Mendelson.

Baehr and Loomis simplify funding options down to four broad categories:

- Create funding through profits (also called "bootstrapping")
- Borrow money through debt (taking out loans)
- Buy funding through selling equity (finding investors)
- Get people to donate money (charitable giving or crowdfunding)

They then dive into five different kinds of equity investors, each with different pluses and minuses:

- **Friends and family** (easy to land, painful to disappoint)
- **Crowdfunding** (platforms that enable many small investors to participate)
- **Accelerators** (not big direct funding sources, but great places to learn/mature and position for funding)
- **Angel investors** (early capital, often with experienced advice attached)
- **Venture capital firms** (increasingly large funding rounds with

high expectations and very active investor involvement)

To raise almost any amount of funding from anyone other than founders (and maybe family), you need to pitch the concept to potential investors and convince them that it's a good investment for them. Baehr and Loomis lay out a 10-slide outline as the core of any good pitch deck:

- Overview
- Opportunity
- Problem
- Solution
- Traction
- Customer or Market
- Competition
- Business Model
- Team
- Use of Funds

Building out this outline into an effective pitch deck is the core of *Get Backed*. If you've never built a pitch deck for investors, I recommend their book. It's full of guidance, instruction, and examples.

Feld and Mendelson cover some of the same basic material as Baehr and Loomis, but mostly pick up where the two Evans leave off. They focus a bit more on venture capitalists than on other types of investors, but cover negotiating, agreeing to a term sheet, creating a capitalization table, and even agreeing to a letter of intent for the acquisition of your business. Their insights are precise and detailed and are intended to accomplish the subtitle of the book: "Be smarter than your lawyer and venture capitalist." If you are pursuing venture capital to scale your business, I recommend *Venture Deals* – read it and refer to it often.

When I say that the next step for new ventures is to develop a Funding Strategy, I really mean develop the strategy and then make it happen. The structure of the Funding Strategy is pretty simple:

The top level purpose explains why you are raising money.

The panorama identifies critical environmental factors that will impact the fund raising:

- How is the economy impacting investor decisions?
- How does your venture fit into current investment trends? Hot or not?
- With whom are you competing in your sector for investment dollars?
- What aspects of your approach/solution will be seen as strengths and which as weaknesses, relative to competing investment opportunities?

The second level of the strategy has three pillars:

- What "sources" are you pursuing — what types of funding sources?
- What "uses" do you have for the money — how are you going to spend it?
- What "returns" do you expect to gain — how will those investments translate into financial gains that ultimately will satisfy those who have invested?

For each pillar, identify three concrete steps:

- For "sources" — what specific investors will you target, how will you gain access to them, and how will you convince them to invest?
- For "uses" — what specific plans do you have for investing the

raised funds: who will you hire, what will you outsource, what will you buy?

- For "returns" — what specifically do you expect from these investments: what metrics, what results, what timeframe?

As mentioned above, your funding strategy likely will change through the life of the venture, so you will create a funding strategy structure like this each time it does.

VisuALS' Funding Strategy

THE VISUALS BUSINESS plan outlined a need to raise $125,000 in initial funding to launch the business. Since customers would pay up-front with a credit card before the product would be shipped to them, as soon as the product launched, cash would start flowing into the business. It was expected that the $125k would get the company to cash flow break even, but another round of funding was scheduled about a year out to fund moving the business off of the OC campus and into a facility that would be able to support growing volumes of orders.

Valuing any pre-revenue business is a challenge. For this reason, many early stage businesses have used convertible notes as the funding source. This instrument technically starts life as debt with all the usual terms (interest, maturity date, etc.) but with the hope and expectation that it will be converted into equity at a future time when there is a credible valuation of the business — typically in the first "real" round of fund raising.

Convertible notes though have their downsides. They can have complicated legal terms, and as debt, they have regulatory requirements that can slow down and burden the funding process. To overcome these challenges, in 2013 Y Combinator introduced (and freely shared) a new investment instrument, the Simple Agreement for Future Equity

(SAFE)[2]. We decided to use this instrument for our initial seed round of funding for the business.

We outlined our funding strategy:

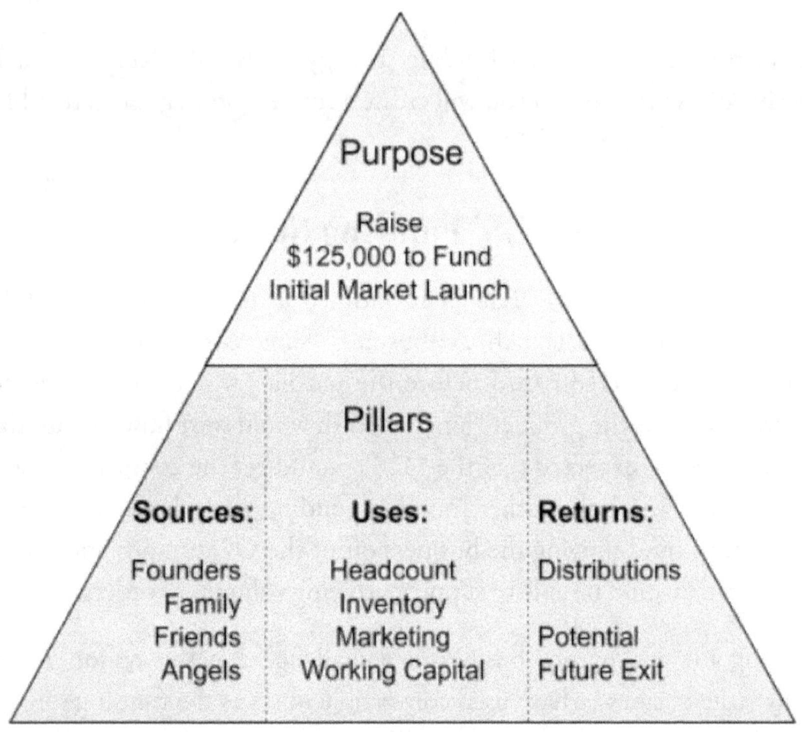

Figure 11: VisuALS' Funding Strategy

Since the VisuALS team had compellingly pitched (twice) to judges in winning the Love's Cup competition, we already had a very strong start to a pitch deck for potential investors. Now we needed to find those investors and convince them to invest.

The timing couldn't have been better. Providentially, OC's annual celebration dinner for its top donors was held the same day as the semi-finals round of the Love's Cup competition. OC's President John

2. https://www.ycombinator.com/documents/

deSteiguer asked if he could tell the VisuALS story at the dinner. He closed the entire evening with the story, including the video of how VisuALS had so dramatically impacted Carl and his wife Janice's life. There wasn't a dry eye in the room. If that wasn't moving enough, President deSteiguer had invited Carl and his family to attend and the VisuALS team was standing behind them in the back of the room. Carl amazingly stood from his wheelchair and walked around to give each member of the VisuALS team a hug.

Figure 12: The VisuALS team with Carl and Janice at the OC dinner

Three-hundred people who had already proven their willingness and ability to open their wallets to support the work of OC heard and felt the impact that VisuALS was having in the ALS community. We were blessed to be able to close most of the seed round of funding from friends, family, and angels in attendance at that OC dinner.

Now we had the MVP, we had the team, and we had the funding.

VisuALS' Market Entry Strategy

VisuALS had reached a critical stage in the startup strategic journey. The company had validated the concept, developed a business plan, raised seed funding, put together a management team, and hired software developers. "All" that was left was to execute.

As a reminder, we had hired four summer interns. We wanted to have students that would be around for a few years, so I went to the professor who taught Programming I and Programming II and asked for a list of the most promising, talented, and flexible programmers from his classes. I researched those he recommended and then reached out to a handful of them. Four signed on: Addison Schwamb, Brendan McKinley, McKenna Gameros, and Preston Seaman.

They were all hourly employees working from their homes during the summer break. I know this approach is going to strike some people as pretty unusual. These were young kids, probably all teenagers, who had just finished their freshman year in college. I don't remember if any of them had ever held a programming job before. Yes, I would regularly check in with them via video conference calls, but they were going to work largely in an unsupervised fashion. Crazy, right?

But this is a model that we'd tried before and it had worked. Most importantly, I knew more about these students than you might think. I trusted the professor who recommended them. Oklahoma Christian University (OC) is a small school, so I simply had to ask others that I trusted. We had another startup[1] already operating on campus, so I asked the developers from that startup if they knew these freshman and what they thought. Many of the developers from both companies lived in the

---

1. https://medium.com/clearpurpose/my-startup-journey-altimeter-software-78b849baa990

honors dorm, so they'd been in each others' rooms or in the common areas of the dorm playing video games and talking about programming projects (for school or for fun) they were working on. I knew well older siblings of two of these developers, so I had a sense of what their life at home over the summer would be like. I had met with each student and learned what they cared about and how they thought. It was a risk, but it was one worth taking.

We met together before the engineering team graduated and before the summer interns officially started, to talk about what needed to be done. We knew that when we launched, we needed three major advances from the minimal viable product (MVP).

The first was the biggest risk to the entire venture. When the engineering students started their project, it was just a (really big) class assignment. They needed to get certain functionality to work to be successful, so they simplified some aspects of their approach. They also had to make some assumptions. One assumption was that patients would need to use a big screen so that they could easily differentiate between the things they were selecting with their eyes. So, they simplified the project by designing it to work on a specific size of large screen. Their hypothesis was wrong. The eye gaze software they wrote actually was quite usable with much smaller devices, and they learned from the MVP that ALS patients required a mobile solution that could be mounted to a wheelchair.

We wanted to officially launch the product at the end of the summer and I thought this one issue could completely derail us. If all the software had to be rewritten to scale to different sized screens, then there was no way it would be working and tested in four months. We had a backup plan that we really didn't want to pursue, but we gave ourselves 30 days. If we didn't make progress on scaling in that timeframe, then we would change directions.

The interns officially started on May 1. About 9 am on that day I got a call from Brendan. He was tasked with taking the main menu screen and making it scalable. He was calling for clarification on how to access the software repository so that he could get to work. I pointed him in the right direction. About 2pm he called again. "Okay, I got that done, what should I work on next?" Wow! What a sense of relief washed over me. The same scalability had to be done to each of the other screens in the product, but at that pace, what I thought might take all summer could be done within a week. We could scrap plan B.

The second and third issues were important, but not enough to keep us from releasing the product. We knew we needed to add a web browser. Addison quickly confirmed that the Chromium browser could be used as a base for developing an eye-controlled browser. We also wanted to add support for many more home automation devices than the engineering team had originally anticipated. McKenna quickly confirmed that the VisuALS system could speak commands to an inexpensive external smart speaker and control a quickly growing list of devices. She specifically tested using a smart remote to control a television, which our first customer, Carl, especially appreciated, and turning lights on and off. Meanwhile, Preston helped work on some of the core operations needs of the business.

Bottom line, the student developers came through like champs!

Jevon, Austin, Steve, and I focused on all the other critical path items — finalizing hardware components, lining up suppliers, determine shipping logistics, setting up an e-commerce website, establishing a customer support infrastructure and processes, etc. Preston Kemp and Tyler Sriver from the original engineering team checked in often in the evenings with the student interns to make sure they had what they needed. It was all coming together. We were building a product and we were building a business as we rushed towards an official launch.

Meanwhile, we continued to be blessed with surprises. The local NBC [2]affiliate had heard about VisuALS and wanted to do a story. We were really pleased how it turned out. And then we started see the same story pop up on NBC affiliates all across the country — from Boston[3] to Honolulu! Sometimes the local station ran the story as is and sometimes they replaced the voiceover with one of their own reporters, but bottom line the VisuALS story was getting out. And then the Today Show[4] called and wanted to do a story. Then Inside Edition[5] called. Then we were featured at ALS News Today[6]. Carl's story especially was resonating with viewers. How providential was our first encounter with him at the ALS support group meeting in January of that year!

What is a Market Entry Strategy?

BY THE TIME A STARTUP gets past the Business Plan and the Funding Strategy, many hypotheses have been tested and refined and decisions made. The final details really come down to product and market. When is the product ready to launch and what is the roadmap for future development? What market segment will you initially target and how and when will you expand to additional markets? What channels will you use to reach that market? What is your pricing strategy? How will you position in the market?

---

2. https://kfor.com/news/

    it-has-given-me-a-voice-again-man-battling-als-receives-help-from-oklahoma-students/

3. https://whdh.com/news/okla-students-develop-speech-device-for-man-with-als/

4. https://www.today.com/health/visuals-technology-helps-man-als-tell-his-wife-i-love-t110845

5. http://www.insideedition.com/headlines/

    23088-new-technology-helps-man-64-tell-wife-i-love-you-despite-als-taking-his-ability

6. https://alsnewstoday.com/2017/05/04/college-students-help-als-patient-communicate-wife/

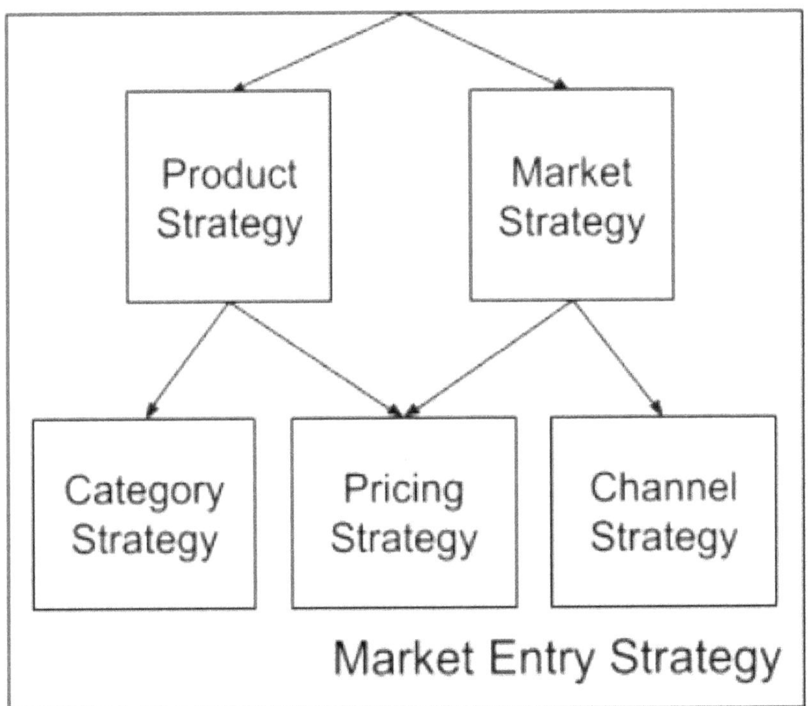

Figure 13: Market Entry Strategy

That last question — how to position, is sometimes specifically phrased as "do we position as a new category?"

For consumers, a product category helps to quickly set in your mind the benefits and limitations of a given product. If you hear that Proctor & Gamble has introduced a new Gillette disposable razor, you quickly have a sense for what that means. Categories are great because they make everyone's job easy. The company marketing a product only has to focus on telling you what is unique about their product within the category, and you, as the consumer, don't have to spend any mental energy learning what the product generically is or does.

But sometimes, a product comes along that is enough different from any of the existing categories that referencing existing categories just doesn't work. These companies start by saying, "Our product is kind of like ______, but it's not." In this case, the marketing team has to work much harder. They can save themselves a lot of effort and money in the long run if they make the investment up front to define a new category. This requires educating the consumer, which is never easy, but once the consumer understands the new category and its benefits, all other marketing efforts become much easier.

The Category Strategy clarifies whether or not a new category is possible or desirable, what the key value proposition is for the new category, and the types of investments that will be made to create the new category in the minds of potential buyers.

VisuALS' Market Entry Strategy

DURING THE FOUR MONTHS that the student interns were readying the software, Steve was readying the hardware, and Jevon was readying our operations. Meanwhile I led the team through the process of finalizing the rest of the Market Entry Strategy.

The initial product was coming together and we had a prioritized list of features the student developers would work on as they had time. Although initially a summer internship, we continued to use student developers (these first four and others) during the school year. We had also negotiated with OC to sponsor an additional engineering capstone project to produce the next major enhancement to the product and we had big concepts for the following year as well.

The initial market was ALS patients and their families, but Austin became very granular in his market planning. He started reaching out to ALSA and MDA chapters across the country to sequence the rollout across different geographies. The business plan called for visiting one city each month, but Austin could get more "bang for the buck" through geographic clusterings and visiting several cities in one trip per month. Austin also started building expertise in Google and Facebook advertising in preparation for the product launch. He also brushed up on his WordPress skills and built the VisuALS website.

Our product positioning was to be "just like" the existing eye-gaze-based speech generating devices on the market, but at a fraction of the price. That defined our Category Strategy and our Pricing Strategy. We were part of an existing category and we wanted the complete solution to have a total cost of less than $3,000.

The Launch

ON AUGUST 31, 2017 supporters and well wishers crowded into The Brew, OC's on-campus coffee shop. OC's President John deSteiguer welcomed guests and then I thanked everyone for their support in getting to this point. During the evening the team packaged up the first system being shipped to a pre-order customer in Houston. We also hand delivered a VisuALS system to Steve and Mary who had driven almost 2 hours from the Tulsa area to pick up the system they had purchased and be part of the festivities, but the greatest highlight was to hear Carl make a speech (with his eyes) about what VisuALS meant to him. You can watch his speech here: https://www.youtube.com/watch?v=xCSb1PyDmjo

That was a very special moment for all of us. Little did we know that just over a week later Carl would pass into glory. We are so thankful for all that he did for us.

And so, VisuALS officially launched. As every entrepreneur knows, that's not the end of the story, but just the beginning. Before long we were fulfilling orders from all across the country. The numbers haven't been huge, but they've been enough to continue to sustain the business and to continue to "love our neighbors by restoring independence, dignity, and hope through affordable assistive technology solutions."

Thank you for joining us on this journey!

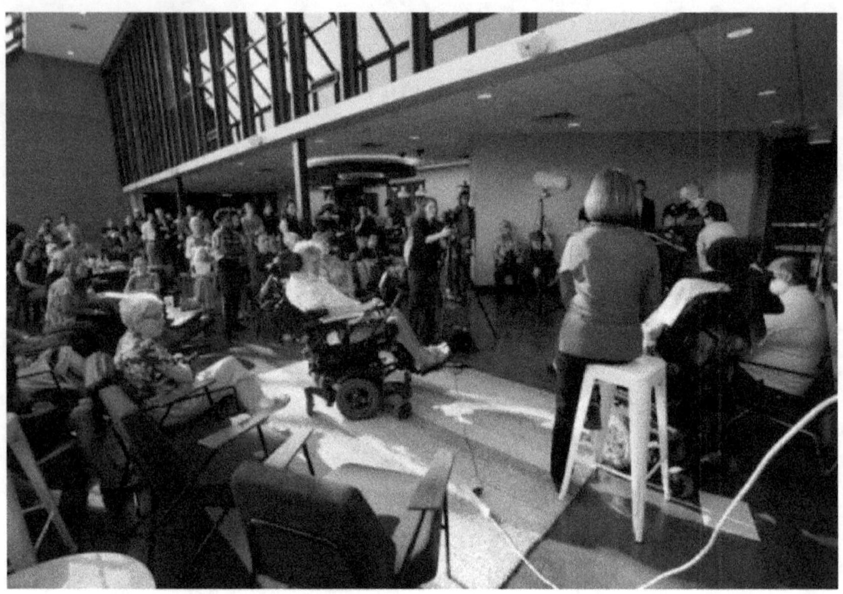

Figure 14: VisuALS Launch Event

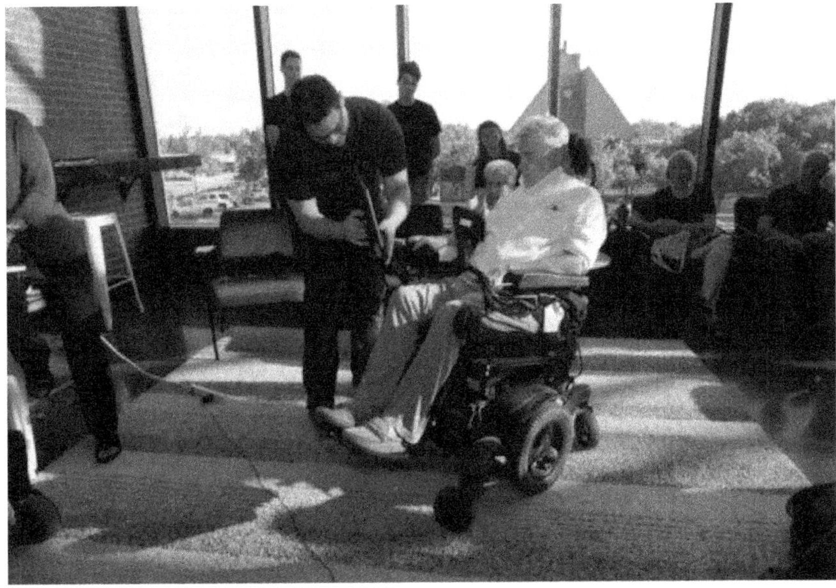

Figure 15: Jevon installing Steve's VisuALS system

Figure 16: Preston, Russ, Tyler, Steve, and Addison with Steve

Figure 17: Preston, Brendan, Russ, and Addison signing the first VisuALS shipment

Figure 18: Austin, Jevon, Preston, Steve, Daniel, McKenna, Brendan, Russ, and Addison with first product shipment

Figure19: Austin, Jevon, Addison, Preston, and Tyler with Carl and Janice

[1] Blank, Steven Gary., and Bob Dorf. *The Startup Owners Manual: The Step-by-step Guide for Building a Great Company*. Pescadero, CA: K & S Ranch, 2012.

[2] Ries, Eric. *The Lean Startup: How Todays Entrepreneurs Use Continuous Innovation to Create Radically Successful Business*. New York: Crown Business, 2011.

[3] Osterwalder, Alexander, Yves Pigneur, Gregory Bernarda, and Alan Smith. *Value Proposition Design*. Hoboken, NJ: Wiley, 2014.

[4] A two-sided business model is one where the company's value comes from connecting two (or more) distinct sets of customers. For example, eBay connects buyers and sellers, Google connects searchers and

advertisers, and Uber connects riders and drivers. In some cases (e.g. Uber) the company is paid directly by the end customer (the rider). In other cases (e.g. eBay) the company collects a transaction fee out of the payment made by the end customer. In other cases (e.g. Google) the end customer (the searcher) makes no direct payment and the company is paid by a third-party (the advertiser).

[5] Osterwalder, Alexander, Yves Pigneur, Gregory Bernarda, and Alan Smith. *Value Proposition Design*. Hoboken, NJ: Wiley, 2014.

[6] A tutorial on developing a Value Proposition Canvas is available at https://medium.com/clearpurpose/whiteboard-tutorial-business-model-canvas-93e92eafdc0e

[7] Adams, Elliott. *The Startup Mixtape: The Guide to Building and Launching A High-Growth Tech Startup*. San Francisco, CA: Startup Mixtape Media, 2017.

[8] Adams, Elliott. *The Startup Mixtape: The Guide to Building and Launching A High-Growth Tech Startup*. San Francisco, CA: Startup Mixtape Media, 2017.

[9] Blank, Steven Gary., and Bob Dorf. *The Startup Owners Manual: The Step-by-step Guide for Building a Great Company*. Pescadero, CA: K & S Ranch, 2012.

[10] Osterwalder, A., & Pigneur, Y. (2013). *Business Model Generation: A handbook for visionaries, game changers, and challengers*. New York: Wiley & Sons.

[11] Loomis, E., & Baehr, E. (2015). *Get Backed*. Harvard Business Review.

[12] Feld, B., & Mendelson, J. (2013). *Venture deals: Be smarter than your lawyer and venture capitalist.* Hoboken, NJ: Wiley.

Don't miss out!

Visit the website below and you can sign up to receive emails whenever Russell McGuire publishes a new book. There's no charge and no obligation.

https://books2read.com/r/B-A-NWOL-WWTHB

BOOKS 2 READ

Connecting independent readers to independent writers.

Did you love *VisuALS: A Startup Strategic Journey*? Then you should read *Six Questions*[7] by Russell McGuire!

[8]

Business success requires making hard decisions. Making hard decisions well requires a depth of understanding about the business and its environment that, unfortunately, many business leaders lack, or at least they haven't formulated their understanding of the business into a framework that makes it easy to consistently and confidently apply.

In this book Russell McGuire asks six simple questions that any leader should be able to answer about their business. The answers to those six questions provide a mental framework that can help leaders navigate the challenges their organizations will undoubtedly face. But more than simply asking the questions, McGuire provides the tools and

---

7. https://books2read.com/u/4XLolN

8. https://books2read.com/u/4XLolN

approaches leaders can use to thoughtfully develop the answers to those questions.

Read more at sdgstrategy.com.

Also by Russell McGuire

A Sprint to the Finish
VisuALS: A Startup Strategic Journey
Six Questions

Watch for more at sdgstrategy.com.

About the Author

Russ McGuire is a trusted advisor with proven strategic insights. He has been blessed to serve as an executive in Fortune 500 companies, found technology startups, be awarded technology patents, author a book and contribute to others, write dozens of articles for various publications, and speak at many conferences. More importantly, he's a husband and father who cares about people, and he's a committed Christian who operates with integrity and believes in doing what is right.

Read more at sdgstrategy.com.

About the Publisher

SDG Strategy helps values-driven leaders of tech-driven startups with the hard decisions they face everyday.

Building and growing a startup is hard. Technology is always evolving, but your values need to be grounded in the unchanging truths and priorities that guide your life. As a leader in a dynamic environment, everyone is looking to you for all kinds of decisions, and few of them are easy. Russ McGuire has been there. Russ brings tools, methodologies, skills, and lessons learned from working with dozens of technology companies over 30+ years.

SDG offers ongoing coaching, strategy lab workshops, online tools, and educational content. Visit us at http://sdgstrategy.com to learn more and to schedule a free 30 minute consultation.